Discover Poetry

(A Selected Madness)

(The illustration on the front cover is by the author)

W. Somerset Maugham: "The crown of literature is poetry. It is its end and aim. It is the sublimest activity of the human mind. It is the achievement of beauty and delicacy. The writer of prose can only step aside when the poet passes."

Contents

1

Within your eyes

Beauty lies
Within your eyes
I can't speak
Of what I seek
Its mystery
A majesty
No purpose seems
To fit dreams
Beneath the lid
Your eyes hid

By Peter Stavropoulos

Ideas:

Beauty as a journey, a tangible experience.

Lid/hid. The ending implies both finding and not finding what you are looking for.

Lies can have two very different meanings. Both could be relevant to a certain extent within the context of this poem. Lies can mean an intentionally false statement, a deception. And lies can mean resides or exists. Beauty resides. Beauty deceives. This poem expresses a dynamic resolution between Beauty and Truth and, in doing so, a passionate love. A surrender to beauty and an understanding of a deeper truth.

Academic Note: From Stanford Encyclopedia of Philosophy – Philosopher Edmund Burke, expressing an ancient tradition, writes that, "by beauty I mean, that quality or those qualities in bodies, by which they cause love."

From The Authour's Website: "Within your eyes" is about discovering that my wife is the most beautiful woman in the world. It was written in response to some unkind words written about her on a poetry website. It is a rhyming poem and took five days to write. With many stops and starts. I knew there was a truth there, but it wasn't until about a year after I had written the poem that I realised that truth myself. The poem led me to what my mind had no hope of understanding on its own.

In the beginning was the Word

In the beginning was the Word
And the Word was Good
And all Spoke the Word
And the Word was Love
And all Loved the Word.

In the beginning was the Word
And the Word became Days
And Days to Life
And Life to Poetry

By Peter Stavropoulos

Ideas:

"And all Loved the Word." The relationship is reciprocal. Love is requited. Suggesting a further relationship between the two.

It was the infinite potential of Words that moved the writer to write this poem.

Loneliness

I could not find loneliness
Because it searched for me
Its thoughts were of happiness
Brought by misery
I could not escape loneliness
Because it found in me
A home of such kindness
It alone could be

By Peter Stavropoulos

Ideas :

The search is a path to Loneliness. Loneliness is the true source of all writing. The writer must find a way within himself. Existence summons kindness.

A quote from philosopher Arthur C. Brooks: "The search for a soul mate is a path to loneliness."

A quote from Ernest Hemingway : "Writing, at its best, is a lonely life. Organizations for writers palliate the writer's loneliness but I doubt if they improve his writing. He grows in public stature as he sheds his loneliness and often his work deteriorates. For he does his work alone and if he is a good enough writer he must face eternity, or the lack of it, each day."

I Thought about you

I Thought about you
And lost my memory
In time
I could not remember
The loss
And yet
In you
I have a memory
Of a happier time

By Peter Stavropoulos

Ideas :

The same person is in a Thought and the cause of a loss of memory.

Beyond forgetfulness a memory of a happier time.

Thought and Memory are disconnected and connected in "you". The poem is a connection to another, happier, time. The passage from Thought to loss of memory is through "you". The passage from now to a memory of a happier time is through "you". "You" is the source of both loss of memory and a memory of a happier time. Implying that "you" is not in the present. The poem was written when the poet was separated from his wife consequently the capital T in thought. Thought was real when she wasn't.

It is not specified that "you" is present in the memory of a happier time. This takes the poem on a further journey. "You" as a conduit to a memory of a happier time. Memory itself having been transported to a happier time.

From The Authour's Website : "I Thought about you" came to me when I was sitting alone in bed one night trying to write poetry. It came to fill the empty space next to me. My wife was in her home country awaiting the granting of a visa to return and live with me. (We had met while she was holidaying on a tourist visa.) Because of the intense drama and uncertainty involved in our separation I had been thinking about her constantly during the whole of this time. I was very lonely, very desperate and I had come to believe totally in the potential of words.

The poet and the rock

The poet and the rock
The rock said
I am a rock
The poet said
I know
The poet and the rock
The rock said
I am a poet
The poet said
I am a rock

By Peter Stavropoulos

Ideas :

The exchange of identities is an exploration of self. Metaphor being part of a greater collective. "The rock" becoming a poet is an ending. "The poet" becoming a rock is a new beginning.

From The Authour's Website : "The rock" had stuck in my mind ever since a conversation I had with a microbiologist many years earlier. The conversation was about beauty. The scientist wanted to make the point that there was as much beauty in science as in the arts. He used the beauty to be found in studying the molecular make up of a rock as an example. I replied that if the rock was a man would he find as much beauty in studying the molecular make-up of the man. I thought that the man as a living being would be much more interesting than any sum of his parts. But that rock has stayed in my mind. Perhaps feeling that I had done it an injustice.

Academic Note : From "Metaphors We Live By" – by George Lakoff and Mark Johnson : Metaphor has been seen within the Western scientific tradition as a purely linguistic construction. The essential thrust of Lakoff's work has been the argument that metaphors are a primarily conceptual construction and are in fact central to the development of thought.

In his words: "Our ordinary conceptual system, in terms of which we both think and act, is fundamentally metaphorical in nature."

Quote : Aristotle : "The greatest thing by far is to have a command of metaphor . This alone cannot be imparted by another;"

The education of the young mind

The education of the young mind
Took place
Behind closed doors
Because that mind –
Initially free –
Had to be
Taught –
The value of freedom.

The education of the young mind
Took place
In an open space
Because that mind –
Once closed –
Had to be
Set free
To explore itself.

By Peter Stavropoulos

Ideas :

Freedom is both acquired and innate. A young mind is one that can be educated. Education being the means by which you learn the value of freedom and are set free.

From "Language, Creativity, and the Limits of Understanding" – by Noam Chomsky : "The creative aspect of language use. The distinctive human capacity to construct in our minds an infinite number of thoughts, expressed in language, and to use them to reveal our thoughts to others in ways that are appropriate to circumstances. And, we could add, to bring them to our own consciousness sometimes and our own understanding. That's actually a crucial, although very little studied topic. One for you students to undertake."

Quotes : William Butler Yeats: "Education is not the filling of a pail, but the lighting of a fire."

Sigmund Freud: "Everywhere I go I find a poet has been there before me."

Joan Didion: on why she writes – "entirely to find out what I'm thinking".

From "A Poet's Advice to Students" - by E. E. Cummings:

A Poet is somebody who feels and who expresses his feeling through words. This may sound easy, it isn't.

A lot of people think or believe or know they feel but that's thinking or believing or knowing not feeling.

And poetry is feeling not knowing or believing or thinking. Almost anybody can learn to think or believe or know but not a single human being can be taught to feel. Why? Because whenever you think, or you believe or you know you're a lot of other people. But the moment you feel you are nobody but yourself. To be nobody but yourself in a world that is doing its best night and day to make you everybody else means to fight the hardest battle which any human being can fight and never stop fighting. …

Let us begin here

Let us begin here
With a sentence
And the sentence is
Love

Let us begin here
With a word
And the word is
Forever

Let us begin here
With a taste of certainty
And the certainty is
You

By Peter Stavropoulos

Ideas :

A moment can seem like a lifetime. A progression can seem like a moment. What starts as a sentence becomes a word. What ends as a word lasts forever. The constant being you.

The art of writing

The art of writing
To one you know
Of the Love you know
Is the art
Of making false
Everything that isn't

By Peter Stavropoulos

Ideas :

The heart guards its secrets well. The lie that was never told hides the truth. The mistake that was never made is the promise that you keep. The love that you give is the hope that you hold.

Quote : Blaise Pascal (philosopher) : "The heart has reasons that reason cannot know."

A Poet's Pleasure

My mind thinks.

My heart knows.

Together, the hand writes, pleasing both.

By Peter Stavropoulos

Ideas :

The hand brings the heart and mind together through words. In equal measure the written word is claimed by both. By writing the hand teaches each about the other without fear or favour.

Quotes : Emily Dickinson : "We meet no Stranger, but Ourself."

Walt Whitman : "Do I contradict myself? Very well then I contradict myself, (I am large, I contain multitudes.)"

By some miracle

By some miracle
I believe in You
The miracle
Of You
By some stroke
Of luck
I found You
To believe in

By Peter Stavropoulos

Ideas:

Choice is not a miracle. To choose to believe is.

Belief is not the miracle. You are.

Quote: Helen Keller: "What I'm looking for is not out

there, it is in me."

The Witch Doctor's Son

He was the first African to do medicine at Oxford. "A bright fellow quite brilliant for a black man" – how he hated those words. He had been top in his class and tomorrow were his final exams. In his room that night he prepared the spell to ensure his success.

By Peter Stavropoulos

Ideas :

The son of a Witch Doctor must learn modern medicine. A black man must overcome prejudice. Embracing who he really is by rejecting the lessons of hate.

From The Authour's Website: About my poem "The Witch Doctor's Son". My local newspaper was running a Short Story Contest. They wanted short short stories of exactly 50 words (not including the title). I decided to enter the contest and sat down to write my 50 word short short story. After about 45 minutes I had completed a short short story of which I wasn't happy with but which satisfied the 50 word criteria. I was tired and walking out of the door of my room when I had the feeling I had to write something. I sat down and wrote "The Undertaker's Widow". It came out fast and in one draft and at exactly 50 words. That was much better than my first attempt, and I thought I was completely happy with it. As I was halfway out the door again another feeling that I had to write something came to me. No words, just the feeling. I sat down and wrote "The Witch Doctor's Son". It came out fast and in one draft, and, as with "The Undertaker's Widow", without any changes and at exactly 50 words. "The Undertaker's Widow" is about my mother, and "The Witch Doctor's Son" is about my father and myself. I was a young man and my father was very ill and near the end of his life when these prose poems were written.

Metaphor

With prose a poetry is as sweet
As Love to air and perfume meet
My second wish came true
My first also was to be with you
As Lovers fall from getting frail
You and I it's true can never fail
We are and never were
Each other's splendid metaphor

By Peter Stavropoulos

Ideas :

One is and isn't the metaphor used to describe one. Can one be and not be when in love? One can if one believes in metaphors hard enough. "Are metaphors real, my love?" "Yes, my love."

Quote : Milan Kundera : "Love begins with a metaphor. Which is to say, love begins at the point when a woman enters her first word into our poetic memory."

My face is not the face you know

My face is not the face you know
It belongs to me
My face is not the only thing I share
I share myself
And the one I Love

By Peter Stavropoulos

Ideas :

Show the world your vulnerability with a look. You're not alone. Don't hide from the focus of their attention. It is up to them to show they care. You can't do that for them.

Quotes : Audre Lorde – "… that visibility which makes us most vulnerable is that which also is the source of our greatest strength."

Bob Marley – "Being vulnerable is the only way to allow your heart to feel true pleasure."

Wish upon

Wish upon
Another's heart
Let her be happy
Let her be strong
Let her Love right the wrong

Wish upon
Another's mind
Let it seek
Let it be free
Let its knowledge find me

Wish upon
Another's soul
Let us journey
Let us travel far
Let our Love guide the star

By Peter Stavropoulos

Ideas:

Written at a time of great uncertainty for the poet and his wife this poem is about finding hope by outlining the future path their relationship will take. Wish upon each other.

"Wish Upon" is a rhyming poem and I felt, as I was writing it, somewhere between prose and poetry. The inspiration behind the poem is expressed in the last line, "Let our Love guide the star". When my wife and I were yet to find security in our relationship, when the height of intensity in our Love for each other coincided with the greatest insecurity from external events, I felt that what we were going through was not limited to us and our experience but was universal, and that elemental forces were at play. Furthermore, that the decisions we made, the faith we kept, influenced those forces. That they were watching us to see what we would do.

2

His Legacy

My Father
Who died yesterday,
Left his legacy
With me.

He knew
That he wasn't going to
"Sleep here tonight,"
And I should have
Listened to him.

But what could I have done
If I had known?
*
One thing that he taught me
Was love.

But I only discovered it
When he died.

One thing that I learnt for myself when he died
Was courage.
*
My Father
Who died yesterday
Left his legacy

With me.
If only I had known about
These things before
Then maybe he wouldn't
Have had to die?
*

But life would have been
Too hard then,
Unbearable,
Too intense.

Every minute painful.

Every second ticking by.

By Peter Stavropoulos

* * * * *

Self-portrait through my father's eyes

I have been out of your life for a long time now.
You have done many things
And I am proud of you.
You have shown the courage I'd hoped you'd have.
The war that beat me
Hasn't touched you.
The stupidity I'd shown, you have learned from.
Good boy.

It wasn't necessary to repeat my mistakes, but we did.
Your mother was a beautiful woman.
I never showed her how much I loved her.
I'm glad you did.
You have also been good to your sisters.
An uncle too.
A father and grandfather.
A husband.
All these things and yet we are still the same
As we have always been.
Before we were born there was another.
I never knew his name.
He was very poor.
I left his poverty for this life.
In my country there are bones everywhere.
Monuments and history.
Blood spilt to defend and to conquer it.
We are both.
I have learned
To fight for what I have.

I have imagined

I have imagined that I will sail across the sea
I have imagined the sea
Sailing too was imagined
I was imagined
And sailing became a hobby

By Peter Stavropoulos

* * * * *

The author imagines himself as a sailor.
An aspiration becomes a hobby.
Life is imagined as something else by someone else.

Like embers for blood

Like embers for blood
Like liquid for paper
Like also for amen
Like justice for all
I am like you
Like paper for fire
Like nothing diminishes

By Peter Stavropoulos

* * * * *

Fire prolongs

What nothing diminishes

In beauty there is myth

In beauty there is myth
I am the brave hero
In Love there is legend
I am the blind storyteller
In truth there is fiction
I am the vagabond poet
In honour there is glory
I am the hopeless romantic

By Peter Stavropoulos

* * * * *

In the unknown I find myself.

Odysseus Translates Richmond Lattimore*

* Richmond Lattimore is an American poet and classicist known for his translations of Homer's Iliad and Odyssey.

Prelude-

Sing o Muse of Pallas Athene's hero
Who journeyed through millennia to a herald's home
Bewitched by the Sirens' song
He had lain shipwrecked on timeless Yesteryear
In battle were gods and men
He prevailed by Wisdom's guile
His story foretold by the ancients
Beauty in a trance would give up her secrets
Sing o Muse of the poet Richmond Lattimore
Who unknowingly became immortal

By Peter Stavropoulos

* * * * *

The Poet is transported by an Ancient Tongue
The Hero is translated into the Modern World
A timeless journey has just begun

The angel that gave me wings

The angel that gave me wings
Said to me
Fly
And I flew
To see
What flying was

The angel that gave me wings
Said Cry
And I cried
To see
What crying was

The angel that gave me wings
Said speak
And I spoke
To see
What I would say

By Peter Stavropoulos

* * * * *

The angel that spoke to me gave me a voice.
Evoking meaning for the two of them.

Love me if I Love you

Love me if I Love you
So too me also

By Peter Stavropoulos

* * * * *

Meaning has life just as life has meaning.

* * * * *

Love me as I love you
Since love enough
Belongs to the
Both of us

* * * * *

From The Authour's Website : I wanted to write a novel. I thought I should. Poetry had always come naturally to me but it was time to progress to fiction. To make something of myself. I sat down to begin my novel and came up with this ten-word poem "Love me if I Love you. So too me also". That, to me, was my novel. It felt complete. But it could only be complete if the words meant something. It had to have characters and a beginning, middle and end. A resolution if they wanted it. And it seemed to me that they did.

Why choose words?

The line doesn't draw itself. I choose instead to follow the contours of her face. A shade of grey against a white background. I use a pencil, my preferred medium. I draw for the love of it. I start at her eyes. The windows of the soul and the centre of her face. My goal is a perfect replica of what I see. What do I see? Lines on paper.

The lines are layered hues to give a three-dimensional effect. The girl in front of me is in a photo. She is beautiful, if only for a moment. She was chosen because she had an interesting face. A face that said something. The eyes say it all, but I continue to the rest of the face to complete a sentence.

I say nothing as I draw. An empty vessel waiting to be filled. 'I've seen her before', I think. Although before is not the right word.

By Peter Stavropoulos

* * * * *

Words are empty without a face to picture
The mind's eye is a reservoir of anonymous images
Each one more perfect than the one before

* * * * *

" ..... Once, in Paris, I got out of the Metro Station and saw suddenly one beautiful face and then another and then another and I tried all day to find words for what that meant to me, and I could not find any words. And that evening there came an equation, not in speech but in little splotches of colour. I realised that if I were a painter, I could found a new school of painting. Painting in splotches of colour. ..... A year later I made this Haiku-like sentence. *'The apparition of these faces in the crowd; petals on a wet, black bough'.* The image is the poet's pigment. The image is not an idea. It is a radiant node or cluster a vortex through which and from which and into which ideas are constantly rushing. It is as true for painting and sculpture, as it is for poetry." ..... Ezra Pound.

3

The Enduring Appeal of the Self-Taught Artist. *

(*A Headline in the New York Times July 7, 2022)

I

A beautiful woman said to me, "Why don't you paint a portrait of yourself?" That never happened. I am a compulsive liar and I've never painted anything in my life. "Why don't you start by drawing yourself and see where that leads you?" I've only ever drawn portraits of famous people and that's led nowhere. Besides, they're much more handsome than I am. "Now you're being falsely modest." A beautiful woman *said* this to me!

You encourage her to see where that leads.

If only I could. I would love to be able to paint. The satisfaction in being able to do something like that would be enormous. I could say I am someone.

"What do you look like?"

Much like any other man.

"Very funny."

I am loving and passionate. Cold and indifferent. Foolish and wise.

"Do you see any future for us?"

Straight to the point, I see. Yes, I only see a future with you.

You busily paint your portrait having never painted before. The brush is steady in your hand and your hand steady on the canvas. You want it to be a kind reflection of who you are, but you can't promise that.

"What do you like doing?"

You are thankful for her questions.

I like sport. I like to dance. I wish I was a better dancer.

"It's fun, isn't it?"

Yes.

"Do you have a girlfriend?"

Only you.

You want desperately not to be alone. The brush is very busy on the canvas.

"How often do you paint?"

Constantly.

"How often is 'constantly'?"

Whenever you're around.

"It seems we have a relationship already."

Doesn't it?

'Why are you painting today?"

I've always wanted to make sense of the world.

"Good for you. And how are you going with that?"

There is only any sense whenever I'm with you.

"I'm glad I can help. When are you with me?"

In my dreams. In my heart. In times of despair and happiness. Whenever I need you.

"You've never grown up, have you?"

I'm a grown man.

"Tell me about your mother."

You already know about her.

"Tell me."

She adored me. She was a simple girl from a rural village and very spiritual. She had a hard life and had formed a relationship with God. She told me she had seen Jesus in a dream, and I believed her.

A beautiful woman is a wondrcus thing. Alluring yet distant. A memory yet very present.

"Is it another day?"

Yes, I have to go to work today.

"I know."

I have to prepare now."

"Enjoy your breakfast"

The day passes. You return from work.

"How has your day been?"

I missed you.

"Tell me a story."

There was a mirror in a forest. No animal saw itself except for the crow. It knew it was a reflection.

"How did the crow feel."

Alone. You know.

"Then why did it look?"

The mirror was there. It was hard to avoid. The poor crow!

"Don't feel sorry for it. It knew what it was doing."

It did.

"Tell me another story."

There was an island with no stairs. You could not climb from the beach to the plateau on top the mountains. You could only see the forest and creatures living there. It means something to me.

"All stories do."

I was happy on the island. On the beach.

"Didn't you wish you could reach that plateau?"

Yes, but I didn't care after a while. I was happy in my little world until ....

"Yes, until what?"

Until I realised there were other people on the beach.

"What happened then?"

The beach wasn't enough. My world wasn't enough.

"Did you try to escape?"

I don't know. I woke up then.

"This was a dream?"

No, it's a made-up story. I never dreamt it.

"What do you hope for?"

Don't ask me that again. I hope only to know you better.

"Tell me another story."

I pretended I could fly once but my wings broke, and I fell to earth.

"But you were pretending. You didn't actually get off the ground."

I couldn't. My wings broke.

"Could you fly if your wings didn't break?"

Yes, in my story I could.

"Where would you fly to?"

To see you.

"I'm here."

But I can't see you.

"Pretend you can."

I do.

"Tell me another story."

You and I are lovers. We are together forever. There is no need to search for you. The search never begins. You have been promised to me forever.

"No search?"

None.

"Forever?"

Yes.

"What does that mean?"

Happiness.

"What does happiness mean?"

To hold you.

"Tell me another story. A good one this time."

There was once a boy and girl, deeply in love, who fought against the world because their love was forbidden.

"I've heard this one."

But do you know what happened to them?

"They died a tragic romantic death."

But before that?

"They lived a tragic romantic life."

There you are wrong. Their life was blissfully happy. They married, had a family and died as very old grandparents.

"Very clever. The tragedy is their death. They were still deeply in love having overcome everything life had thrown at them. I'll give you that one."

You tell me a story.

"I'm good at that."

Go on.

"Once upon a time."

My favourite way to start a story.

"Once upon a time there lived a shoemaker. On the outskirts of the village lay his little shack, just before the deep dark forest."

Sounds familiar but I like it, go on. Was there a wicked stepmother and innocent young children?

"The shoemaker lived alone but wanted so much to get married and have a family."

Boring! Who would want to live in a shack on the edge of a deep dark forest? Okay, I get it. Love is special.

"What about you?"

I have you.

"Yes, you do."

Does love last?

"Tell me a different story."

A black girl and a white boy loved each other. They loved each other in spite of the prejudices of their community. She, a simple girl from a village back in the 'old country' and he, a former wannabe ladies' man.

"Like you?"

No, not like me. I was never a ladies' man. I don't need anyone else, I have you.

"Do you?"

Do you want me to finish the story? Anyway, the two of them fought these prejudices while trying to make sense of their love.

"Was it complicated?"

It was. This wasn't their first relationship and they had both been hurt. Were the people against them in the right? Did they have the right to love? Did they deserve love?

"It's a birthright that has to be earned sometimes."

Who's telling the story? It was their birthright, but it had to be earned.

"Did they succeed? Did they earn it?"

They couldn't do it themselves, no matter how hard they tried. The world was against them, and they were against each other. But they worked it out by letting go.

"Yes?"

By letting go of who they thought they were. They realized that their love belonged to no one else. They were who they were only as part of a whole. It was the start of overcoming the hate around them and in growing together. And so they lived happily ever after in the shack by the deep dark wood.

"That's my shack.

The deep dark wood too.

"I own it."

You seem to be everywhere. Were you ever with me in my previous marriage?

"You were right the first time. I am everywhere."

Did I fail or did you let me down?

"You had the same chance as you have now. But it seems you needed to learn something."

Have I learned my lesson? Am I a good boy now?

"You were always a good boy. It was just that you wanted more. I couldn't help when you wanted more. I only have enough to give."

That sounds like a country and western song.

"Some of my best work."

Whose turn is it to tell a story?

"It's your turn again. You need to do better than you have if you want to hold my attention."

What about the story of the owl and the pussycat?

"I haven't heard that one for a while."

The owl and the pussycat went to sea to see what they could find. To find. To find. To see what they could find.

They found each other without any bother at the end of a pea-green boat. They did. They did. At the end of a pea-green boat.

What did they find? A kind of love. They did. Find a kind of love. They did. They did. A kind of love.

"Love is kind" said the owl to the pussycat. "What a find," said she. All there on a pea-green boat. To sea to see. All there on a pea-green boat.

"I'm going to cry. The owl and the pussycat were two lost romantics. Poor kids."

You're the hopeless romantic of all hopeless romantics.

"That's me!"

You tell me a story, it's your turn.

"When one loves one dies when one dies one loves."

Morbid!

"To love someone, you die and give birth anew."

Ok, getting weird.

"The new 'you' lives forever in love."

That's a happy ending I believe.

"I'm a happy person."

It's not really a story though.

"It could be."

Go on.

"There once was a man who tried to find love. He was born to find it. But in this life, it can be hard to find.

He found true love with the girl of his dreams, but true love didn't find him. It didn't last. She left him for another life, and he searched again.

In his way were others searching for the same thing. But only one is meant for you. This time he found true love despite the obstacles. His heart led him to where his head could not go."

You're full of cliches.

"So I am."

That story sounded like my life but I'm over it now.

"The heartbreak? The searching? The need for love?

Exactly.

"You're a tough guy now."

I sure am.

"Show me. Tell me a story."

There once was a man who wrote about his life. His marriage. His love. His children. His ambition. His failures. His successes. His happiness. His sadness. By writing about them he became less real. Once removed from events, like a photo captures the moment at the cost of living that moment. The expression of life becomes the life. The capturing of life becomes that life.

The depiction of his world became his world. His feelings saw themselves thereby losing real feeling. He became lost in his art. Replacing life with art. The fantasy becoming himself. No longer real. He was what he imagined himself to be.

You ready yourself for another day at the office; the morning commute takes you into town. The job you do will give you the capacity for leisure.

I am no hero.

But you continue to write when you get home.

I belong in the too hard basket.

Words are your friends. They are sympathetic.

I don't deserve them.

You are becoming the hero of your own story again.

"Tell me your own story."

You know it better than I do.

"Go on. 'Once upon a time ......'"

Once upon a time there lived an old man who was young and a young man who was old.

"In the same house? There weren't one and the same, were they? I've heard that one."

They each promised the other wisdom in exchange for company.

"Did they get their wisdom?"

Yes, in the bucket loads. They became friends. One helped the other and vice versa.

"Like you and me?"

We're friends.

"Yes, we are. But you do forget me sometimes."

You make friends again with your imagination. The only true friend you ever had. Talking incessantly about 'old times yet to come'.

"What do you want from our relationship?"

Peace.

"Don't you have it already?"

It's fleeting. Now I see it, now I don't.

"You know I can only do so much. I might not be the answer."

I know you're not the answer, but you're the only answer I have.

"Maybe I'm the cause of the problem? Give me up and see."

I need to hold onto something.

"Maybe you should let go?"

You are me letting go. I let go through you while holding on for dear life to everything else.

"We are a complicated pair, aren't we?"

Does it have to be complicated?

"If you don't let go".

Are you just the product of my imagination? If so, we really should say goodbye.

"Goodbye."

Fleetingly you feel anxious. You cannot be alone. And alone you are, for as long as you keep away from her.

"Find and you shall seek."

Shouldn't that be "Seek and you shall find?"

"What are you looking for?"

I should ask that. "What am I looking for?" I'm looking for something real.

"I know you are. You've been looking for that for a long time."

You are a precious. You know you are precious but that doesn't stop you. If you have to be a precious little thing to find what you are looking for, then so be it.

Don't you have what you are looking for? Isn't it 'find and you shall seek?'"

I suppose I have. I believe in what I am doing.

"The ambition?"

I'm not ambitious.

"Are you not!?"

If I achieve what I want to achieve without any recognition I would be happy. I'm not ambitious. What people think is not the most important thing to me.

"You are very ambitious. To achieve something worthy of being ignored! You're the most ambitious person I know."

You need to get out more.

You try to write something worth reading but you get back to her and being the hero of your own story.

"How are you darling?"

Exhausted!

"You should take a break."

You take a break from writing and from her. Living your life away from her you feel very healthy. Very happy. Very content. You also know it won't be long before you are back to her. Being content is the first step to being not content. The top of the hill before the downhill race to the bottom. The first one there gets the "prize"!

"Find and you shall seek. Know and you shall journey. Be free and you shall let go. See and you shall look."

The words at the end of each sentence are you.

"Hear shall and I tell me. You a part of be let me. Anymore to be alone need don't you? Sacred is too secret no. Surprise can nothing. Blasphemy only is the to lie. Nothing conquer the world conquer. Reward its own patience being you wait."

Your imagination is your biographer. You cannot be wrong if you exist.

Picture a paint. Wall the on it hang. Story tell your picture the let.

By Peter Stavropoulos

Walt Whitman – "Every hour of every day is an unspeakably perfect miracle."

www.ingramcontent.com/pod-product-compliance
Lightning Source LLC
Chambersburg PA
CBHW040743250626
47164CB00001BA/20